TOP TEN PARIS

A Complete best of Paris short stay Travel
Guide for Tourists with Insider Tips

(pocket travel guide)

Artus Rodrigue

Introduction

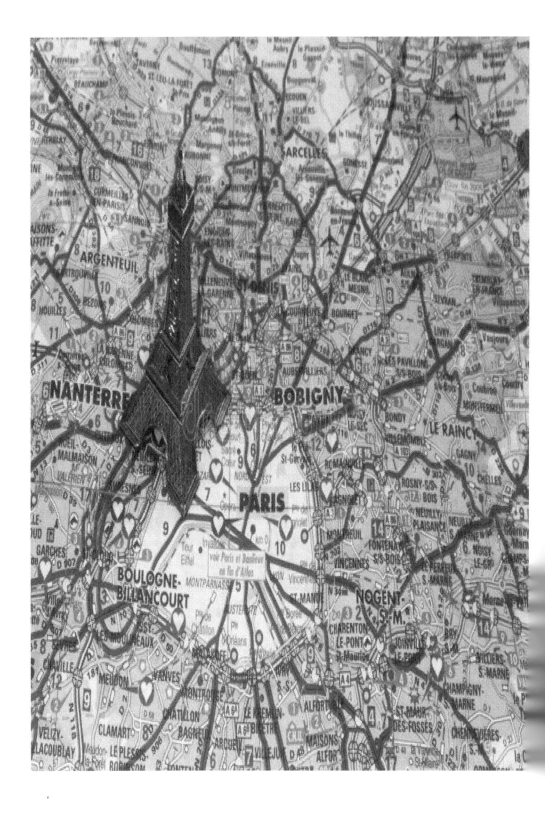

Chapter 1

Visiting Paris as a tourist [things you should know]

France's metropolis and capital, Paris, is located in the north-central region of the nation. By around 7600 BCE, people were living in the current city's location, which is situated along the Seine River some 233 miles (375 km) upstream from the river's mouth on the English Channel (La Manche). From the island (the Île de la Cité), the present metropolis has extended well beyond both sides of the Seine.

One of the eight départements that make up the administrative territory of the Île-de-France, Paris is located in the center of the prosperous agricultural region known as the Paris Basin. It is without a doubt the nation's most significant commercial and cultural hub. Region: 41 miles (105 km) squared; 890 square miles for the metropolitan area (2,300 square km).

Population(2022): 2.14 million

City's personality

Paris has long been regarded as one of the most significant and alluring cities on the whole globe. It is valued for the possibilities it provides for business, commerce, education, culture, and entertainment; in particular, its cuisine, haute couture, artwork, literature, and intellectual community have an exceptional reputation. The nickname "the City of Light" (la Ville Lumière), which it acquired during the Enlightenment, is still apt since Paris continues to be a major hub for learning and intellectual pursuits.

Paris's location at a pivotal intersection of marine and land routes important to both

France and Europe has had an ongoing impact on its development. The original location on the Île de la Cité was chosen as the capital of the Parisii tribe and area under Roman rule in the first century BCE. By 494 CE, the Frankish monarch Clovis I had conquered Paris from the Gauls and established it as his capital. Hugh Capet (reigned 987-996) and the Capetian dynasty solidified Paris' dominance, making it the political and cultural center as modern France took form. Since France has traditionally been a highly centralized nation, Paris has come to be associated with a strong central government that attracts a large portion of the intellect and vigor from the regions.

The Seine separates the three major areas of old Paris. The Île de la Cité, the location of both ecclesiastical and temporal power, is located in its center (the name "cité" refers to the center of an old city). The Right Bank (Rive Droite) of the Seine holds the center of the city's economic activity, while the Left Bank (Rive Gauche) has historically been the home of intellectual life. However, these divisions have become fuzzier in recent years. All of these roles were combined in the heart of France and subsequently in the heart of an empire, creating a very essential setting. The years 1358, 1382, 1588, 1648, 1789, 1830, 1848, and 1871 are remarkable for such incidents; yet, in this context, the emotional and intellectual atmosphere that was generated by rival forces often provided the conditions for significant violence in both the social and political spheres.

Paris has mostly kept the early city's circular form throughout its centuries of expansion. Its bounds have widened to include the neighboring towns (bugs), which are often constructed around monasteries or churches and frequently serve as markets.

 The city's expansion was mostly eastward from the middle of the 14th to the middle of the 16th century; since then, it has been westward. It is divided into 20 arrondissements (municipal districts), each with its mayor, town hall, and special characteristics. The numbering moves from the center of Paris to the extreme east in a spiral pattern like a snail's shell. The first, second, third, and so forth arrondissements are referred to in French as the premier, deuxième, and so forth. The massive urban agglomeration is the result of adaptation to urbanization's issues, which include zoning, housing, social infrastructure, public utilities, and immigration.

Landscape

Metro area

The Seine, Oise, and Marne rivers pass through the Île-de-France area, which includes Paris. Large beech and oak woods surround the city; they are known as the "lungs of Paris" because they serve to clean the air in the highly industrialized area. No area of the city proper is more than six miles ten kilometers from the plaza in front of Notre Dame Cathedral. The surrounding heights have been acknowledged as the city's boundaries since it sits in a depression created by the Seine. The elevation ranges from 85 feet (26 meters) in the Grenelle district in the southwest to 430 feet (130 meters) at Montmartre Butte in the north.

The city's center and 10 of its 20 arrondissements are traversed by the Seine over a distance of around 8 miles (13 km). It moves from the southeast corner of the city to the northwest, then gradually bends southwest until exiting Paris at the southwest corner. As a consequence, what was once the east bank of the stream changed to its north bank and ended up becoming its west bank; as a result, the Parisians adopted the straightforward, immutable designations of Right Bank and Left Bank (when facing downstream).

However, specific locations are often denoted by an arrondissement or a sector (quartier).

At water level, which is about 30 feet (9 meters) below street level, the river is lined with cobblestone quays decorated with trees and bushes, at least on the parts that haven't been turned into expressways. Another row of trees may be seen slanting toward the river from the roadway. The retaining walls between the two levels are typically constructed of large stone blocks and are embellished with the large iron rings once used to moor merchant ships. Some of the walls are also pierced by openings left by water gates for former palaces or inspection ports for subways, sewers, and underpasses. The walls are sometimes covered with ivy.

The broad waters of the Seine and its tree-lined banks create a garden effect, giving the impression that Paris is a city with plenty of greenery. Numerous public parks, gardens, and squares are scattered throughout the city, along with tens of thousands of trees (mainly plane trees with a few scattered chestnuts) that border the streets. On the territory that used to be set aside for the monarchs outside of the ancient city, the majority of the parks and gardens of the present core city are located.

The Bois de Boulogne and the Bois de Vincennes, two historic royal military preserves at the entrances to Paris, were transformed into "English" parks under Napoleon III, who had been inspired by London's parks while residing in Britain. Additionally, a significant portion of the landscape was transformed into promenades and garden squares under his rule. The local administration began initiatives to develop additional parks under Mayor Jacques Chirac in the late 20th century, and similar projects continued into the 21st century.

In the 12th arrondissement (municipal district) of Paris, on the right side of the Seine River, the Promenade Plantée is a partly elevated parkway constructed over an abandoned rail line and bridge. It was the first elevated park in the world and the first "green space" built on a viaduct (the first phase finished in 1994). Other cities have subsequently been inspired by it to convert abandoned train lines into public parks. Between the Opéra Bastille and the Bois de Vincennes, the total feature is around 4.5 kilometers (nearly 3 miles) long. The Viaduc des Arts, which runs alongside Avenue Daumesnil, is situated below the elevated part. The old archways now house specialized businesses.

Weather in Paris

Paris benefits from the mild Gulf Stream effects and has a comparatively moderate climate due to its position on the western edge of Europe and in a plain that is quite near to the sea. However, the weather may be highly unpredictable, particularly in the winter and spring when the wind can be brisk and chilly. The average temperature is in the lower 50s F (about 12 °C) year-round, the upper 60s F (about 19 °C) in July, and the upper 30s F (about 3 °C) in January. Every year, for around a month, the temperature dips below freezing, with snow falling on about half of those days. The city has implemented efforts to reduce air pollution, and a water filtration system has rendered tap water safe for consumption.

Societal culture

Paris has long been recognized as the major cultural center of the Western world, drawing in thinkers and artists, and serving as a hub for new ideas and the supremacy of art. This idea was particularly true in the early 20th century when the city attracted many authors and artists from other countries, notably Amedeo Modigliani from

Italy, Ernest Hemingway from the United States, James Joyce from Ireland, and Pablo Picasso from Spain.

The city's cultural life is still quite vibrant and unique, despite some critics' claims that Parisian culture has shifted toward spectacle over genuine originality. The theaters and music halls, museums, art galleries, and art cinemas are always packed with people because Parisians appreciate novelty, have an abundance of intellectual curiosity, are devoted art supporters, and know how to dress up even the most basic cultural event with flair and elegance.

The Comédie-Française, the Odéon Theatre, and the National Theatre of Chaillot are the three main state-run theaters, and they all present a variety of French classics, serious current plays, and international imports. The many privately owned "boulevard" theaters, which struggle to exist, provide lighter content. More than 150 smaller theaters, many of which get state funding, provide a variety of experimental "fringe" performances, cabaret, and other types of entertainment. Several little "art" houses show a broad range of films, many of which have subtitles, in addition to numerous multiscreen commercial movie theaters. The majority of France's film studios are in the Paris suburbs.

The National Museum of Modern Art at the Pompidou Centre, the Orsay Museum of 19th-century art and culture, and the science museum in La Villette are some of the more recent, notable museums. The Louvre is still the best of the traditional art museums. The organization of large, elaborately decorated exhibits, often retrospectives of a single artist or historical era, is a specialty of Paris.

After the early 1970s, the city's once-moribund musical scene became considerably more vibrant, thanks in part to assistance from the state. Through the 1989 inauguration of a second opera theater at the Place de la Bastille, the city also reaffirmed its devotion to opera. The Music Festival (Fête de la Musique), which takes place in June, and the Autumn Festival (Festival d'Automne), which runs from mid-September to late December, are two significant yearly events that emphasize music and theater.

Chapter 2

France's travel restrictions

France has officially lifted all Covid restrictions on overseas passengers as of today, August 1st, 2022. Travelers will no longer need to test before arrival as the nation fully reopens.

Additionally, travelers will not be required to provide documentation proving they have recovered from Covid-19 or that they have had a vaccination. Travelers may enter and exit the nation as they did before the outbreak without needing a "compelling cause" to do so.

This is fantastic news for tourists who want to have a wonderful vacation in France. We can only hope that this marks the end of all Covid restrictions in the nation.

The French government has the authority to implement "emergency brake" measures for up to two months in the event of a new variety or a major rise in cases even if all Covid restrictions have been lifted as of today. Until January 31st, 2023, this "emergency brake" contingency is in effect. The administration cannot reinstate measures beyond December 31 without legislative consent.

Europe and France Open

The decision by France to remove all Covid limitations is one step closer to removing restrictions from all major European destinations. The last two significant locations in Europe with active Covid protocols are the Netherlands and Spain. Both of which continue to demand confirmation of vaccination for visitors from certain nations.

After two years of additional travel precautions, things are starting to return to normal. As it happens, tourists will undoubtedly look for nations that have completely revoked their Covid regulations. Many tourists have encountered difficulties due to the expense of testing, the lengthened lines, and the overall inconvenience of limitations. Tourist numbers in nations with them still in place are probably lower than in those without them.

Generally speaking, traveling is simpler.

Without Covid limitations, traveling will be simpler, but passengers need to be aware of the French airport delays. For instance, just 38% of flights at Paris' Charles De Gaulle Airport (CDG) operated on time between July 1 and July 10. It appears that this is becoming the new standard while flying. The aviation sector is under a lot of stress due to a lack of qualified employees and rising demand.

Keeping Out of Chaos

It should be mentioned that over the same period between July 1 and July 10, Orly Field Airport (ORY), located near Paris, saw 79% of its flights run on time. If given the option, passengers traveling into ORY will be more likely to have a positive experience. Knowing which European airports are the best for avoiding flight delays is crucial since the differences between airports may have a big influence on travel. Taking advantage of fast-track entry while entering France is another method visitors may avoid standing in line. France currently makes use of its Parafe Electronic Gates to let some non-EU nationalities enter the country. Passengers may use the gates to enter France without conversing with border officials. Since the lines are often shorter and move more quickly, the reduced wait times are the procedure's most important advantage. The system is currently accessible to tourists from the United States, Canada, the United Kingdom, and several other nations.

Tourists adore France

France, and Paris in particular, has long been a popular travel destination. With 11.2 billion views as of May 17th, 2021, a TikTok poll just found that Paris was the 6th most watched location on the app. Airlines have taken note of the rising interest, and to capitalize on the attractiveness of the location, France's French Bee Airline has introduced $281 nonstop flights from Miami to Paris. Beginning in December, there will be three weekly departures from the airport.

A World After Covid

Travelers are more ready than ever to get back to the way things were before the epidemic as France, Europe, and the rest of the globe begin to open up without limitations. Even while personnel shortages and supply chain problems continue to pose challenges for certain areas of travel, the removal of limitations has made it simpler for everyone to travel. The benefits of the ongoing global reopening will be felt by passengers, employees, airports, and airlines.

Chapter 3

Ten things to know before visiting Paris

Living in Paris teaches you how to live like a local. There are certain behaviors you pick up and others you don't. However, all of these "rules" apply to both residents and guests. So have these ten things in mind the next time you visit Paris:

1. **Avoid gambling and street commerce**

On several tourist streets, notably the small cups game, I often see people gambling. This is a scheme to defraud you of money. I know it appears like fun and is somewhat innocuous, but a few individuals are collaborating to give you the impression that it is secure. Do not participate in these games; you will just waste your money!

2. **Avoid butting out in public**

Don't discard your cigarette on the sidewalk if you smoke. Recently, new legislation was implemented to stop individuals from hurling their cigarette butts into the streets. Put them in the garbage. If a police officer observes you doing anything else, you will be fined 68 euros. That cigarette is incredibly pricey!

3. **Steer clear of eateries in popular tourist areas**

Restaurants in highly frequented areas are often not the best. You may rely on travel guides to direct you to excellent eateries that are hidden gems. Restaurants around the Arc de Triomphe, Notre Dame, and the Eiffel Tower may seem to be traditional French eateries, but they will cost you a lot for a subpar meal.

4. Avoid purchasing bread or croissants from large chain supermarkets.

You are aware of the bread French people eat! But have faith in them. They do not get their bread from large chains or supermarkets. They get their baguettes and croissants from neighborhood boulangeries and patisseries. And here's a tip to assist you to figure out whether the product you're purchasing was indeed produced inside the bakery: The foods are freshly produced inside, not frozen if it reads "artisan Boulanger" on the front window!

5. Stand straight

Because many of us in Paris are eager and like to move quickly, it is customary to stand to the right of escalators so that people may rapidly ascend them on your left.

6. Steer clear of pricey roofs

Avoid pricey roofs and hunt for hidden jewels instead, such as the George Pompidou Terrace or the Printemps Terrace, which both provide 360-degree views for no charge. Avoid climbing the Eiffel Tower and instead look for less costly places with greater views, such as the top of the Arc de Triomphe. We all want to see the Eiffel Tower in a picture of the Paris skyline, so it's touristy and a little disappointing.

7. Steer clear of upscale coffee shops

Avoid upscale coffee shops where the prices are simply too high. Instead, look for little cafés in less popular areas. The price will be far lower, and the coffee could even be better! And at many cafés, if you sit near the counter, your coffee will only cost you one euro!

8. Pick up a few French words.

People in Paris are polite. not all of them, at least. They just admire your attempt to speak a few words of French. We are expected to speak English, just like when we go to the US. A simple "bonjour" or "merci" demonstrates your effort. And we are grateful!

9. **Be prepared for August.**

The city has a terrific feeling since you feel like you have it to yourself if you visit Paris in August when everyone is on vacation. But keep in mind that many stores and restaurants will be closed at that time. However, it's not always a terrible thing. It forces you to go off the beaten path in search of an open, decent restaurant.

10. **Continue walking.**

When possible, choose to walk rather than use the metro. You could be pleasantly surprised by the charming stores, little streets, and amazing architecture you might have missed if you had just taken the subway.

Chapter 4

Where to stay in Paris

(The best neighborhoods and hotels)

Paris. The Light City. Finding the perfect spot to stay might be difficult for first-time visitors since the city has 20 arrondissements (neighborhoods), amazing historic sights scattered throughout, and dozens of hotels, hostels, and flats to pick from.

I've stayed in every neighborhood and a variety of lodgings throughout my several trips to Paris (as well as my few months spent living there). Each neighborhood in Paris has a distinct character, as well as advantages and disadvantages. One must constantly make a trade-off in this situation.

I've put up this thorough information on where to stay in Paris to assist you in deciding where the best spot to stay for your trip is. I've given a quick overview of each place, explained why I prefer it, and listed my top lodging options there.

Arrondissements

First District: Louvre

Bourse, 2nd Arrondissement

Third District: Temple

Hôtel-de-Ville, 4th Arrondissement

Panthéon, 5th Arrondissement

sixth district: Luxembourg

Palais-Bourbon, 7th Arrondissement

Élysée, 8th Arrondissement

Opéra, 9th Arrondissement

Entrepôt, 10th Arrondissement

Popincourt, 11th arrondissement

Reuilly, 12th Arrondissement

Gobelins, 13th Arrondissement

Observatoire in the 14th arrondissement

Vaugirard, 15th Arrondissement

Passy, 16th Arrondissement

Batignolles-Monceau, 17th arrondissement.

Butte-Montmartre , 18th arrondissement.

Buttes-Chaumont , 19th arrondissement.

Ménilmontant, 20th Arrondissement

Where in Paris is the greatest area to stay on a tight budget?

For vacationers on a tight budget, Montmartre is one of the city's least expensive areas. Some of the nicest city views can be seen from this 18th arrondissement location (especially at sunset).

Which area in Paris is ideal for families?

Families on the road will appreciate Montparnasse's peace and affordability.

What area of Paris is ideal for first-time visitors?

Stay in the Le Marais if it's your first time visiting Paris.

What area in Paris offers the greatest shopping?

The world-famous Champs-Élysées is known for its upscale shopping. The world's top brands are all available here. It's in the 8th arrondissement of Paris.

What area of Paris has the finest nightlife?

One of the greatest areas to stay in if you want to party and experience Paris' nightlife is Le Marais. It is situated in the 4th arrondissement and is surrounded by fantastic cafés, eateries, and stores. A fantastic nightlife can be found in Bastille as well.

What is Paris's overall finest district?

My favorite Parisian areas are the Latin Quarter and Le Marais. Both cities have a ton to offer tourists in the way of attractions, dining options, and attractive neighborhoods. Remain there!

Following that, the following summary of the major arrondissements will help you choose the ideal area for your trip:

Overview of Paris's Neighborhoods

Bastille (11th)

Spanish Quarter (5th)

Champs-Elysées (8th)

Marais, Le (4th)

Montmartre (18th)

Isle of the City/Louisiane (4th)

Montparnasse (14th)

The Halls (1st)

Saint-Germain-des-Prés (6th)

Belleville (20th)

Champs de Mars and the Eiffel Tower (7th)

Bastille (11th arrondissement)

The name of this area, which spans the 4th, 11th, and 12th arrondissements, comes from the renowned jail that formerly stood there (the storming of which started the French Revolution in 1789). The jail is no longer there, and this vibrant and energetic neighborhood is now recognized for its hip pubs and clubs that cater to young Parisians.

I'd suggest staying in this arrondissement if you're seeking a good time. The narrow cobblestone streets and convenient location make it seem quite Parisian.

The best hotels in Bastille

Budget: Auberge Internationale des Jeunes (International Youth Hostel) - Although this hostel is secure and well-kept, the utilities are modest. There isn't a kitchen where guests may prepare their meals, but there is a microwave, and complimentary breakfast is offered every day from 7 am to 9:45 am. In addition, there is a safe place to store baggage and a common room with vending machines where people prefer to hang out. You must be younger than 30 to stay here since it is a youth hostel.

MID-RANGE: Paris Bastille is a classy, peaceful hotel with soundproofed rooms and spacious walk-in showers that is situated immediately across from the Opera House and close to the Gare de Lyon. Additionally, they provide a daily breakfast buffet and complimentary WiFi.

LUXURY: Hôtel l'Antoine - This 4-star boutique hotel was once a monastery in the 17th century, but its contemporary design has wacky wallpaper and brilliantly patterned cement tiles. Here, no two rooms are similar. A snack bar, lounge, and daily complimentary breakfast are also available. A sauna and cold shower are also located in the fitness center!

Spanish Quarter(5th arrondissement)

One of my favorite parts of Paris is the Latin Quarter, which is surrounded by little squares with cafés and small alleyways that bend at odd angles. It always seems like you are traveling back in time a few hundred years while I am here exploring. It is situated in the 5th arrondissements and is in a busy area. You'll be in the center of the activity even if it's not as quiet as other parts of Paris since there are so many eateries, pubs, and jazz clubs there

The best hotels in the Latin Quarter

Budget: Young & Happy Hostel - This hostel has a sizable cooking area, modest but clean showers, and rather basic rooms with comfortable mattresses. The common area is a nice and unusual place to hang out since it is an ancient basement with stone walls. There are daily happy hours for meeting other tourists, and sometimes the staff may offer evening activities. A complimentary breakfast of pastries, coffee, and juice is also available.

MID-RANGE: Hôtel Minerve is located within a beautiful Haussmannian structure from 1864 with flower-adorned balconies on a peaceful street close to Notre Dame and the Sorbonne. The inside of this building has just undergone renovations to add appeal, featuring exposed stone walls, visible beams, and unique artwork throughout. A sizable center courtyard is also included. Each morning, a respectable breakfast spread costs nine euros, and an airport shuttle is available (not free).

LUXURY: Grand Hôtel Saint Michel - The Jardin du Luxembourg and the Panthéon are only a short stroll from the Grand Hôtel Saint Michel. Even though it mostly serves business visitors, it isn't stuffy, and the location is unrivaled. Numerous upscale amenities are available on-site, including a hammam, fitness center, spa, and concierge.

Champs-Elysées(8th arrondissement)

The most well-known and affluent boulevard in Paris is dotted with theaters, cafés, high-end specialized shops, well-known chain restaurants, and large department stores. It's a fantastic spot to shop and take pictures during the day, or to hit the clubs at night. It's in the 8th arrondissement. The neighborhood that surrounds the street is among the most affluent and lavish in all of Paris.

It's extremely calm if you keep away from the main street. Although it's conveniently placed and lovely, there aren't many "interesting" things to do around. Additionally, the cost will rise.

The best hotels in Champs-Élysées

BUDGET: BVJ Champs-Elysées - Having been functioning since 1948, this hostel in a former home is one of the oldest in Paris. Each morning, they provide a complimentary French breakfast, free bag storage, and a beautiful, quiet garden where guests may relax.

MID-RANGE: The contemporary, spotless, and trendy rooms of the Hôtel Magda

Champs Elysées. The bar is a great place to work while enjoying a beverage (or some complimentary coffee). They also provide smartphones so that you may stream Netflix and make free calls. There is also a wonderful courtyard here.

Marquis Faubourg Saint-Honoré is a luxurious hotel. The rooms include marble fittings and clawfoot bathtubs, and they are comfortable (if not a little bit undersized). The breakfast is pricey, so skip it.

Marais, Le (4th arrondissement)

Le Marais, which translates to "the marsh," has recently undergone revitalization and is now a fashionable, vibrant neighborhood with trendy art galleries, shops, and cafés. Many museums may be found among the historic buildings, half-hidden courtyards, and narrow, twisting lanes. Here, you'll also discover some of the city's top eateries and pubs. My favorite part of Paris is there.

Several homosexual pubs, cafés, and stores can also be found here since it is the epicenter of LGBT life in Paris.

The best hotels in Le Marais

Budget: MIJE Marais - This is a special hostel since it consists of three refurbished buildings from the 17th century: MIJE Fourcy, Fauconnier, and Maubuisson. The rooms are quite modest, but there is a lovely outdoor courtyard, free breakfast, and free Wi-Fi.

MID-RANGE: Villa Beaumarchais - The Opéra Garnier and Place de la Madeleine can both be reached on foot from this quaint and charming hotel that is located on a quiet side street. As a result of the abundance of wood furniture and flowery wallpaper, the rooms have an ancient air to them. It's quite comfy. Opt for a room that has a view of the inside courtyard. Along with free Wi-Fi, a fitness facility, and an American-style breakfast buffet, they also provide these services.

LUXURY: Place des Vosges, one of the most beautiful and historic squares in the world, is home to Pavillon de la Reine. Beautiful rooms with old furniture, large windows, and stunning, distinctive décor can be found in the structure covered in vines. On-site amenities include a spa and a fitness facility. This is a lovely small retreat. Fun fact: Queen Anne of Austria did visit this location. If you want to treat yourself, have dinner at Restaurant Anne.

Montmartre (18th arrondissement)

Montmartre, which has long been the home of hungry artists, provides a breathtaking panorama of the city. Cobblestone streets, hip cafés, pubs, and the lone vineyard in the city are all found in this neighborhood. Even if some of its former splendor has been lost, it remains one of Paris' hipper neighborhoods.

Due to the much lower rents here than elsewhere in the city, it is also home to a large number of students. Due to the high concentration of visitors and students that often occurs at night, it is also rather noisy. If you're searching for a calmer place to stay, consider staying on one of the lovely side streets.

The best hotels in Montmartre

Budget-friendly Le Village Montmartre by Hiphophostels is close to pubs, restaurants, and supermarkets. It has a view of Sacré-Coeur and is a tiny, charming hostel. Each morning, a French breakfast is available for 6 EUR, or you may use the spacious kitchen to prepare your meals.

MID-RANGE: Le Relais Montmartre is a hotel in Montmartre that is located in a quiet lane. With exposed timbers and antique furnishings, the rooms have a rustic appeal and are quite affordable. If you want to splurge, check out the breakfast; it's excellent, and the subterranean restaurant is special.

LUXURY: Terrass" Hôtel - The hotel bar offers breathtaking views of Paris and the dramatic setting sun. The rooms are more spacious than most in town and feature lovely interior design in a traditional Parisian flair. Yoga lessons and spa services are available at the hotel. Breakfast on the patio is a must.

Île Saint-Louis and Île de la Cité (4th arrondissement)

The historic heart of Paris is located on these two islands in the Seine. In 52 BC, the Romans established a camp on the island that is today home to Notre Dame, Sainte-Chapelle, office buildings, and the

Conciergerie. Also, it's constantly crowded and quite noisy.

On the other hand, the wealthy and influential of Paris reside in the peaceful Île Saint-Louis area, which is full of beautifully maintained old buildings and streets. Stay here if you desire luxury and peace. There aren't much else but posh hotels.

Île de la Cité and Île Saint-Louis' best hotels

Budgets: HA! This place doesn't have that!

MID-RANGE: Given that it is located on Île Saint-Louis, the Hôtel De Lutèce in Notre Dame is surprisingly inexpensive. It has many homey features, like functional fireplaces, despite being on the smaller side. There are just 23 rooms, yet every one of them is soundproof and air-conditioned. It has a homey vibe as opposed to a motel.

LUXURY: Hôtel Saint-Louis en L'Isle – This hotel is housed in a townhouse dating back to the 17th century that still boasts a lot of its original elegance, including exposed stone walls and wooden beams. The rooms are opulently large. You'll feel like royalty staying at one of the area's most opulent hotels. Even breakfast is served in the basement with the stone vaults.

Montparnasse (14th arrondissement)

One of the most contemporary areas of Paris is Montparnasse, which has many more office buildings, brand-new residences, and a more neighborhood-like atmosphere. Montparnasse, which is situated in the 14th arrondissement next to the same-named railway station, offers cheap lodging options and a big selection of eateries. Although it is less classically attractive than other areas of the city, it is also considerably more "local" and less expensive.

The best hotels in Montparnasse

Budget: FIAP Jean Monnet; this is more akin to a hotel conference center than a party hostel since it often hosts school groups. It's in a peaceful area. You cannot, however, bring your food inside (they check!). Only those ages 18 to 30 may live in dorms.

MID-RANGE: Novotel Paris Centre Gare Montparnasse – This cozy, chain hotel is designed for business travelers and has all the amenities you would anticipate from a chain. Memory foam mattresses and spacious walk-in showers are features of the rooms. It is sleek and well-lit. If you have children, they will like the balloon creatures the staff makes, and they also provide complimentary coffee and tea.

Luxury: The beautiful Niepce Paris Hotel is a modest boutique hotel. Since the hotel is very new, everything is still gleaming. Even the junior rooms are contemporary and elegant, and some of them have patios outside with jacuzzi tubs. The restaurant offers distinctive French-Japanese fusion food.

The Halls (1st arrondissement)

Les Halles (pronounced lay-AL), which served as Paris's primary market until it was demolished in 1971, is the focal point of this posh, vibrant area. For many years, the market served as "Paris's gut." There is now an underground mall, and the streets are lined with artisanal food stores, coffee cafes, and designer boutiques. Staying here puts you in the middle of all the activity (the mall receives around 150,000 visitors each day!).

The best hotels in Les Halles

Budget hotel Hôtel de Roubaix provides exceptional value and is within two minutes from the metro. The rooms are clean and big, and it is just 1.5 kilometers from the Louvre. A continental breakfast is also provided. Nearby restaurants and cafés abound, and the staff is quite welcoming.

MID-RANGE: Hôtel du Cygne - When you stay at Hôtel du Cygne, you'll feel like family. It has a very DIY/homey vibe to it since all of the bed linens and drapes were hand-sewn by the owner's mother. This hotel is small, with just a few little rooms, but it's a cozy place, and it's close to the Etienne-Marcel Metro Station. Every morning, breakfast is served (which you have to pay for).

LUXURY: Novotel Paris Les Halles - What's not to love about air-conditioned rooms, round-the-clock room service, and huge beds? In addition to being close to major retail districts like Rue de Rivoli, Novotel Paris Les Halles is also accessible by foot from the Louvre. You may relax in the lounge after a day of exploration or enjoy classic French cuisine or beverages on the gorgeous terrace.

Saint-Germain-des-Prés(6th arrondissement)

In the past, Saint-Germain-des-Prés was a haven for creative people. It is now one of Paris' priciest and trendiest districts. Celebrities, expensive art galleries, fashionable stores, and upscale restaurants are now located in the area.
Although lodging there is not inexpensive, the neighborhood is lovely to stroll over. It is just what you envision Paris to be.

Favorite lodging options in
Saint-Germain-des-Prés

Budget: Hôtel de Nesle - There aren't many places to stay in this area of the city, sadly. Nesle is the spot for you if you like kitsch! There is rarely a wall in the whole building that is unadorned. While some rooms have common bathrooms with showers, some have private facilities. You may unwind in the inside garden.

MID-RANGE: Hôtel Moderne Saint Germain is a chic boutique hotel with air conditioning and colorful accents throughout each room. There are little balconies in some rooms. Breakfast is also excellent here.

LUXURY: Hôtel Récamier - The staff there helps set up any activities you'd want to go on, and the free afternoon tea is a great touch. The structure is old and gorgeous, the rooms are big and air-conditioned (I like the beds).

Belleville (20th arrondissement)

Undoubtedly, one of the grittier areas in the city is Belleville. It has a bustling Chinatown and resembles a mingling of several cultures. Belleville, the hub of Paris's immigrant population, is steadily gaining popularity with hipsters and younger children due to its lower cost.

This area has some of the greatest ethnic cuisine, a fantastic street market, and is close to the Le Marais, where you can always go for upscale French cuisine. More and more often, I choose to stay in this area of town.

the best hotels in Belleville

Les Paul is a rather new hostel with a great chimney lounge and a rooftop area. It's always enjoyable to visit the bar/restaurant on the ground level since it's well-liked by both residents and groups. The mattresses are comfortable, and the rooms are quite contemporary. One of my favorite places to stay in the area; every time I organize a meet-up in Paris, it generally takes place here.

MID-RANGE: Hôtel des Pyrénées - Although this hotel doesn't particularly stand out, it just underwent significant renovations, resulting in sleek and contemporary rooms at a reasonable price. Additionally, there are family rooms for up to four people, making it an affordable choice for families.

LUXURY: Hôtel Scarlett - A chic, newly renovated hotel with breathtaking interiors. Each room has a flat-screen TV and a spacious, comfy bed. They have a helpful concierge who can guide you around the city and help you organize your vacation.

Champs de Mars and the Eiffel Tower (7th arrondissement)

As you may have predicted, if seeing the famous Eiffel Tower is your major motivation for visiting Paris, you should be at the Eiffel Tower/Champs de Mars (and have easy access to some other huge attractions). In addition to the stunning architecture, there are several excellent museums of natural history and contemporary art, as well as the vast Parc du Champ-de-Mars. The 7th arrondissement is a bustling, touristic (read: pricey) neighborhood to stay in, yet it's unbeatably convenient!

Best hotels near the Eiffel Tower and Champs de Mars

Budget: 3 Ducks Hostel boasts one of the greatest sites in Paris, just a 10-minute walk from the Eiffel Tower. The staff is helpful, the accommodations are compact yet cozy, and the showers are spotless. This hostel has newly updated furnishings and is posher. It is among my favorites in the city as well.

MID-RANGE: Hôtel Eiffel Kensington - A basic hotel that offers private single rooms at reasonable costs and is located close to the Eiffel Tower. Although the rooms are on the smaller side, they are nonetheless plenty large and have a small desk. It's an affordable choice for the area.

The Pullman Paris Tour Eiffel offers luxurious accommodations with contemporary, minimalist rooms that include leather furnishings and chic finishings. Usually, there is a workstation and a small sofa. A pretty excellent eating deck and a fitness center are also available. Every room has breathtaking views of the city, and some have balconies that look out onto the tower.

You won't go wrong staying anywhere in Paris, no matter what you decide. There is no such thing as a terrible eating area, and every location is lovely (after all, this is Paris!). It is conveniently linked by metro.

The Latin Quarter, Saint-Germain-des-Prés, Bastille, and Le Marais are my picks for the top four Parisian areas to stay in.

But there is something in every neighborhood for someone, so choose the one that best meets your requirements. I guarantee you won't be let down!

Chapter 5

Ten Best Restaurants in Paris

New to Paris? And you are wondering where to find the best restaurants to eat savory Paris meals then this chapter got you covered.

1. Tawlet Parisian

11th Arrondissement (Folie-Méricourt)

Kamal Mouzawak, a social entrepreneur and food activist, founded Lebanon's first farmer's market and several farmer's kitchens. He has now taken a variation of the idea to Paris. Tawlet Paris, a two-level cafeteria and grocery store with the same emphasis on regional Lebanese foods served buffet-style, is situated a block from the Canal Saint Martin. With meals of the day provided for weekday lunch, you may sample cuisine from the Beqaa Valley, Mount Lebanon's region, or the south, depending on the day. On Saturdays, brunch is dominated by the diverse tastes of Beirut, with dishes like Moujadara, Manousheh, tabouleh, kibbeh, and the greatest knafeh in town—a sweet cheese confection drenched in syrup. You may take home a variety of Lebanese wines, spices, and other pantry necessities.

2. Bouche

The 11th Ward (Folie-Méricourt)

Some would even argue that there are too many genuinely outstanding wine bars and caves à manger (customers must purchase food to drink) in the 11th arrondissement. Despite its short nine-month history, this small dish and natural wine bar seem completely new. That might be due to the interior's vaguely Brutalist design, which is more typical of Berlin (exposed textured stone, picture windows, vintage furnishings, and minimal decor), or the restaurant's inventive seasonal menu, which rotates every two weeks and is paired with specialty drinks and European grower wines. Recent highlights include skate fish simmered in a Thai bouillon with lime, garlic, and chile pepper and octopus okonomiyaki coated in lardo. Whatever the motivation, it's a wonderful addition to a vibrant area for food.

3. Caf Luce

Montmartre

Even before the pandemic, there was a movement in restaurant styles and menus in favor of revitalized classics. Due to the upheaval of the previous two years, customers' yearning for familiarity has become even stronger, and some of the city's best chefs have answered the demand.

Before opening Pouliche, her first solo restaurant in the shadow of the Gare de l'Est, chef Amandine Chaignot worked in Paris and London for the greats, including Passard, Piège, Ducasse, and many more. Her cooking is creative and fun there, and she loves to experiment with unusual taste combinations. But with her most recent endeavor, Cafe de Luce, she puts a modern twist on a time-honored eating idiom: the bistro.

This all-day café-bistro named for Chaignot's grandmother rules over the Place Charles Dullin in front of the Théâtre de l'Atelier in Montmartre. It serves everything from spruced up devilled eggs with wild herbs and pickled onions to beef tartare that can be topped with Sturia caviar if desired and savory croissants with ham and comet or smoked salmon alongside a mound of frisée. A vegan main dish option is also a permanent feature on the menu, another indication that the Parisian restaurant is changing. Generous salads are also available.

4. Collier of the Queen

Enfants-Rouges

Few locations in Paris are as distinctive as the one inhabited by this brand-new seafood bar-restaurant on a prominent North Marais corner. Diners enter through the bar, where high communal tables and stools remain open to walk-ins and serve natural and biodynamic wines alongside a short menu of briny bar snacks. From there, they proceed through a slightly larger restaurant space with moody lighting, tables covered in pressed white linens on one side, and retro booths next to wall-length mirrors on the other.

You can view the whole menu there, which includes a variety of meat choices, line-caught fish, mixed seafood platters, and a massive onion soup encased in puff pastry that is already trending on social media.

You may enter the subterranean wine cellar and liquor store, which is open till late, by making your way around the far back (you can also stay for a drink, sans corkage fee). Go for lunch to sample the restaurant's daily special for a different atmosphere.

5. Café Lignac

Gros-Caillou

While many of the city's revival bistros offer new takes on traditional cuisine, Café Lignac remains adamantly sentimental. This 7th arrondissement institution, formerly known as Café Constant, was taken over by chef and TV celebrity Cyril Lignac (France's equivalent of Jamie Oliver) from the adored chef Christian Constant, who has formally retired his apron and sold off all of his locations. Many aspects of Café Constant, like the zinc bar, the stone walls and gilded moldings, and even certain dishes, such as the cassoulet with duck confit and sausage, remain the same.

What has changed is that Lignac has added certain 19th-century dishes to the menu, like the vol-au-vent de ris de veau, the white tablecloths are back, and the bistro seats and façade have a forest green tint (sweetbreads in a hollow puff pastry shell with wild mushrooms). For dessert, you have two options: you may choose a variety of contemporary pastries from Lignac's network of pastry shops, or you can stick with tradition and choose a flawlessly cooked Tarte Tatin served with crème crue or a hearty baba au rhum (a Lignac hallmark).

6. Substance

Chaillot

The 16th arrondissement, located in the westernmost part of the city, has previously been considered something of a dining wasteland, unnoticed by renowned chefs and restaurant groups and including only basic bistros, corner cafés, pizza places, and local bakeries. Then this swanky neo-bistro appeared, bringing with it a young, creative chef and an innovative eating experience to liven up the surroundings.

Whether you make a reservation for lunch or evening, Matthias Marc, one of the most promising young chefs in Paris, draws heavily on his Jura heritage to create a tasting menu (five, seven, or nine dishes) that is bright and flavorful. In one dish, there can be potato emulsions with trout eggs and pickled onions, while in another, there might be grilled duck with chou kale, broccoli, and pickled cauliflower.

Anselme Selosse, the fourth-generation producer of Jacques Selosse, one of the most prestigious and highly ranked champagne houses (which gives more context to the restaurant's name: it's an homage to Selosse's small batch premium cuvée), put together the selection of 180 cuvées from notable champagne houses and small producers. The food alone is reason enough to make a reservation, but bubbly gets a special mention.

7. Le Mary Celeste

Marais

Sometimes it's better to leave things alone. That includes Brittany oysters, a signature plate of deviled eggs filled with sesame mayonnaise and topped with fresh ginger, shallots, deep-fried wild rice, and spring onions, as well as a sharp selection of grower champagnes, craft cocktails, and Deck & Donohue beers that never leave the menu at this well-liked natural wine and small plates bar in the North Marais. Beyond that, locals and visitors frequent the restaurant for its consistently changing menu of inventive dishes (recent examples included fried Padron peppers with anchovies and a Cascabel salsa and Sichuan-braised beef cheek with eggplant and kumquat) as well as its weekly wine tastings with small producers.

8. Balagan

Location Vendôme

This gorgeously built shrine to modern Mediterranean food a block from the Tuileries Gardens is one of the most genuinely enjoyable and refreshing places to eat, noon or night. Assaf Granit and Uri Navon, two of Jerusalem's top chefs, opened the first of several restaurants in Paris, Balagan, in 2017.

With its rich mash-up of flavors (Israeli cuisine incorporates a variety of influences, including Syrian, Greek, and Lebanese), and festive atmosphere (it's not uncommon for diners and staff to end the night dancing on tables), Balagan quickly became a hit. Sharing of meals like a deconstructed kebab, veal kubenia, Fattoush salad, and grilled lamb is encouraged whether you're eating alone or with a party, but you shouldn't feel obligated to divide the two wonderful pieces of bread between the menu, the brioche-y Kubane, and the crispy Frenavon.

9. The Argent Rotisserie

De La Tournelle Bridge

La Tour d'Argent, the most renowned restaurant in the city, is not accessible to everyone, and even if it were, it will be closed in April for a nine-month refurbishment. Thankfully, its sibling establishment across the street concentrates on classical rotisserie meals and traditional bistro fare, offered in a setting that generally only exists in exotic imaginations (think: red checkered tablecloths, ruby red leather banquettes, and vintage wine bottles displayed as decor).

The menu includes hearty main dishes like beef rib for two with béarnaise sauce and crispy fries and milk-fed lamb shoulder braised for five hours in rosemary, as well as spit-roasted half chicken from a family-owned farm in northern France, served with luscious mashed potatoes and pigeon served with carrots and thyme (in other words, vegetarians beware). The ancient wine cellar of La Tour d'Argent, one of the largest in the world, guarantees that there will be a fine wine selection.

10. Biedercafé

Marais

No, Paris was not the birthplace of the crêpe, but this family of cafés offers the finest of Brittany to the city. With more design-focused interiors, what started as a modest, rustic shrine to organic buckwheat galettes and delicious crêpes in the Marais has now spread across Paris (and beyond: the creator Bertrand Larcher has created branches in Cancale and Japan, where the firm began 25 years ago).

Anywhere you go, you can discover more creative takes on the classic "pancake," including herring with Saint-Malo potatoes, smoked salmon with ikura salmon roe, crème fraîche, and dill, and for dessert, a rolled crêpe with white chocolate mousse, matcha tea, and strawberries. The use of premium ingredients, such as Bordier butter and locally grown fruit, sets these crêpes apart from the competition.

Chapter 6

Ten top shopping malls in Paris

If you are looking for where to get the best shopping experiences in Paris, then these listed malls are elite for you.

1. The Four Times

Since 1981, the Quatre Temps, the biggest mall in Europe, has ruled over the La Défense neighborhood, only ten minutes by Metro or RER from the heart of Paris.

Due to the diversity offered by its 230 shops, the enormous 130,000 m2 shopping mall is currently separated into four floors and draws large crowds of customers. In the airy, expansive mall, many of the big French and international businesses are present. Along with well-known ready-to-wear fashion brands including American Vintage,

Claudie Pierlot, Comptoir des Cotonniers, Maje, Lacoste, and Uniqlo, it is home to popular cosmetics companies like Sephora, Lush, Mac, and Kiko.

Not to mention the gigantic Apple Store for IT fanatics and the Fnac multimedia store. There's a good chance that this is what you're searching for.

It is accessible every day between 10 a.m. and 8.30 p.m.

2. La Defense

The highest and most recognizable buildings in France are located in this business district, which is mostly surrounded by towers, corporate headquarters, and offices: Coeur Défense, EDF, Granite, and First.

The neighborhood includes the modern church Notre-Dame de Pentecôte, two metro stations, the "Les Quatre Temps" shopping center, and other buildings. The spectacular Grande Arche, a masterpiece created in 1989 by architects Johan-Otto Von Spreckelsen and Paul Andreu, is the main landmark of the neighborhood. Three communes make up La Défense, the largest commercial hub in Europe: Courbevoie, Puteaux, and Nanterre.

On the esplanade, in the center of this contemporary setting, 60 works of art enliven this frame. The Lower Esplanade Charles-de-Gaulle square's "The Dance," a collection of 35 carved planters stretching across 3,600 square meters, Shelomo Selinger's "Fantastic Characters," Joan Miró's "The Monumental Fountain," Alexander Calder's "Red Spider," a 15-meter-tall sculpture near the Total Tower, Yaacov Agam's "The Monumental Fountain," and "Takis Basin," a man-

3. The Halls

The biggest shopping center in urban areas is Westfield Forum des Halles, which has 150 shops. Among the many fashion companies included are Aigle, Calzedonia, Celio, Claudie Pierlot, Comptoir des Cotonniers, du Pareil au Même, H&M, Lacoste, Levi's, Etam, Gap, Mango, Naf Naf, Petit Bateau, Pimkie, Princesse Tam Tam, Promod, Sandro, and Zara.

Of course, there is the iconic Centre Pompidou, which resembles a futuristic large chain store and makes me think of the film Brazil. Children often like this fountain, which was designed nearby by Jean Tingley. Brancusi's Studio is another obscure subterranean site that is sometimes disregarded. By buying a ticket from Pompidou, you may enter the reconstructed museum.

The magnificent canopy over the shopping center is one of the city's newest attractions. The Les Halles neighborhood is thriving and vital to the city. The Louvre, Notre-Dame Cathedral, the Centre Pompidou, and Le Marais are all within easy walking distance. The whole area will be the beating center of the city once the current improvements are done. Due to its proximity to the Louvre and other attractions, as well as the various restaurants and bars in Les Halles and the Marais, the area has several hotels, making it one of the best places to stay.

It is open from 10 am to 8 pm, Monday through Sunday.

4. The Three Quarters

Aux Trois Quartiers was a department store in Paris that was opened in 1829 at the intersection of Rue Duphot and Boulevard de la Madeleine. Early in the 20th century, the company employed postcards that were printed with the name and address of the shop for promotion reasons. In the 1990s, the shop was renovated into a commercial hub.

There are fifteen shops selling clothing, perfume, and cosmetics. 10 a.m. to 7 p.m., Monday through Saturday, 21 Avenue de la Madeleine (Arr 1) Madeleine metro station.

To restore the grandeur of this Department Store created in 1932 by Louis Faure-Dujarric and to provide a more effective layout, Sébastien Segers and Laurent Goudchaux decided to combine the historical narrative with a modern design. They have offered a novel interpretation of the facade's grid and guiding principles, including design rationalism, horizontal stripes, straightforward geometrical forms, sizable display windows, and noble materials. The gaping angle leading to the basement store has been replaced with a fully circular entrance. To make it easy to understand the volumes, the building's ductwork, construction, and circulation system have all undergone rigorous evaluation.

5. Grand Boulevards Les

In Belle Époque Paris, the Grands Boulevards were the place to be seen and be seen: at the cafés, the theatre, or in the majestic coverts (glass-roofed arcades that served as the first malls in history). You can practically see the Grands Boulevards as they were captured by the Impressionists in their paintings, complete with well-dressed Parisians strolling through broad avenues lined with shops, cafés, and horse-drawn carriages, all against a background of opulent Haussmannian grandeur. The Grands Boulevards, which include the renowned department shops Galeries Lafayette and Au Printemps next to Place de l'Opéra, continue to be the city's primary shopping district despite the presence of chain stores, street vendors, and fast-food establishments.

Along with being a popular destination for shopping, the Grands Boulevards are also home to the magnificent Opéra Garnier, which Napoleon III commissioned. The region is also home to some of the city's best small museums, many of which were formerly private collections housed in hôtels particuliers (mansions) from the 19th century and are worth the trip alone. An incredible collection of Italian Renaissance art is housed at the majestic Musée Jacquemart-André, while the poignant Musée Nissim de Camondo honors the tragic demise of one family. A magnificent collection of Asian art may be found in the Musée Cernuschi, while the Musée National Gustave-Moreau honors the Symbolist master.

6. The Madeleine

A parish church of the Archdiocese of Paris, Madeleine hosts daily Masses, various religious gatherings, as well as weddings and funerals. The Church's basement houses the Foyer de la Madeleine (entry on the Flower Market side). A three-course French dinner is served by volunteers beneath the vaulted ceilings of the Madeleine, like many other foyers run by religious and civic organizations around France, for a small yearly membership fee. At a lounge at the other end of the lobby, one may get one of Paris' cheapest espressos after dinner. The Foyer walls are often decorated by local artisans.

The Madeleine was built in the Neo-Classical style and was modeled by the much smaller Maison Carrée at Nîmes, one of the best-preserved Roman temples. One of the first significant neoclassical buildings to imitate the whole external form of a

Roman temple rather than just the portico front was this one.

The church's interior consists of a single nave with three domes over large arched bays that are lavishly gilded in a manner influenced by both Renaissance artists and Roman baths. At the rear of the cathedral, above the high altar, is a statue by Carlo Marochetti that depicts St. Mary Magdalene being lifted by angels, evoking the custom of ecstasy that she experienced in her daily prayer when she was alone.

7. The Lafayette Galleries

A renowned high-end French department store and a shopping center with hundreds of brand names are called Les Galeries LaFayette. Many visitors stop by the main shop in Paris to check out the gorgeous art nouveau interior design. A massive Christmas tree is kept within a magnificent dome in the center of Les Galeries LaFayette throughout the holiday season. Many people visit this location for the expansive city views and the famous fashion shows that often occur. A wonderful department store in Paris, Galeries Lafayette is renowned for its designer clothing, fine dining, Art Nouveau architecture, and in-store activities. Even today, Galeries Lafayette is a well-known Parisian shopping center. The store's architecture has made it a popular tourist destination, and it offers in-store events including monthly Paris fashion shows and courses on how to make macarons.

On Boulevard Haussmann, the original flagship shop now spans three structures. In addition to more than 50 Galeries Lafayette stores around France, there are two more store locations in Paris (one on the Champs-Elysécs and one in Beaugrenelle). The store also has several foreign locations.

8. The Season

Le Printemps Haussmann is a large department store and shopping center that has everything. Many visitors compliment the shopping center's convenience and cleanliness, saying that it's simple to buy a souvenir for everyone. Shops provide a wide range of goods, including designer clothing, high-end goods, custom tailoring, and beauty and wellness products. Originally built in 1923, the tearoom has a stunning vaulted ceiling with spectacular stained glass decorations.

One distinctive feature of the Haussmann Store is the spectacular dome that sits above the main restaurant and was built in 1923. The cupola was dismantled and stored in Clichy in 1939 to protect it from being destroyed during air strikes. The grandson of the original designer utilized blueprints preserved in the family business's archives to rebuild it in 1973. In 1975, the cupola and building's façade received historical monument status. Their famous jingle from 1996, "Au Printemps, we avons les vêtements!" is sung in advertisements.

The Printemps store is situated on Boulevard Haussmann in the 9th arrondissement of Paris, along with other well-known department shops including Galeries Lafayette. There are further Printemps stores in Paris and other French cities. The company has constructed stores outside of France in Andorra, Shanghai, the Ginza shopping district of Tokyo, and Jeddah, Saudi Arabia.

9. The Champs-Elysées

The Place de la Concorde and the majestic Arc de Triomphe are separated by more than two kilometers of this old route. The Champs-Élysées was once a marsh, despite being called "the world's most beautiful avenue." The Sun King's gardener, André Le Nôtre, tracked its first path in the 17th century. A legend developed as a consequence. The avenue becomes more beautiful as the years go by. The headquarters of several prestigious companies are located in this well-known region. Since 1913, Guerlain has had its headquarters here in a historically significant building. To the delight of visitors, the Louis Vuitton flagship, which is nothing short of a monument to luxury, also functions as a contemporary art museum.

High-end American jewelry retailer Tiffany & Co. just built a location on the renowned Paris Avenue. It is a sister store to the main location on Fifth Avenue in New York and it is where the Audrey Hepburn movie Breakfast at Tiffany's takes place! Other well-known manufacturers of fine jewelry and timepieces, like Cartier and Mauboussin, are also represented on the street.

Foodies will find many treats to sample on a stroll down the Champs-Élysées: there is a Ladurée, famous for its mouthwatering French macarons, and 86 Champs, a cutting-edge concept store developed by a partnership between Pierre Hermé and L'Occitane, offers a singular sensory experience fusing fragrance and pâtisserie.

10. Village of La Vallee

Shopping in La Vallée Village is unlike anywhere else.

It is open every day of the week and about 40 minutes from Disneyland and Paris. The days are unique in La Vallée Village. More than 120 shops from some of the most intriguing French and international designers can be found in La Vallée Village, which sells large items from previous seasons at competitive rates all year long. The Village offers the most amazing shopping days with five-star elegance to make your holiday special, and it's just 40 minutes from Paris.

The Bicester Village Shopping Collection 11 unique European and Chinese destinations are included in the Bicester Village Shopping Collection, all of which are close to some of the most significant gateway cities in the world: London, Paris, Shanghai, Milan, Dublin, Barcelona, Madrid, Brussels, Antwerp, Cologne, Düsseldorf, Munich, Frankfurt, and Suzhou. The Collection stands out for its uncommon brand mix, breathtaking settings, rich cultural diversity, great service, and savings.

Chapter 7

Top ten places in Paris for sightseeing

Are you looking for places to visit in Paris, France? You'll be ready to go when you read my list.

One becomes humble when they travel because they realize how little their position in the world is. As you may already be aware, France's capital and the most populated city is Paris. It's interesting how many activities there are to do in Paris.
As of 2014, this enormous city's capital welcomed over 15.6 million international visitors. Paris is one of the top tourist attractions worldwide because of its amazing art, culture, and way of life.

This ought to at least give you a hint of Paris' notoriety and its suitability as a tourist destination. The capital is well endowed with antiquities, museums, and art galleries as well as breath-taking scenery along the rivers, beautiful landscapes, and museums.

No matter what time of year or season a tourist arrives, there is always something to do and somewhere to go. You can picture what a fantastic trip it would be to spend time in Paris.
The many popular museums in Paris are what make it famous across the globe.

Walking through ancient streets and walkways and taking in some of the biggest historical relics is a wonderful pleasure. However, Paris is a very big and crowded city.

As a result, you'll require a thorough understanding of some of these locations since relying entirely on your expertise may make things look challenging. And even if you do not intend to visit Paris any time soon, reading this book might still help you be ready for it.

1. French Tower

Paris would not be the same without the iconic Eiffel Tower. It was created by Gustave Eiffel to mark the French Revolution's 100th anniversary and shown at the Exposition Universelle in Paris in 1889. It is one of the most popular tourist attractions in the world, drawing about 7 million tourists a year to its 324-meter height.

The Eiffel Tower 58, which has two stories and rises 58 meters above the ground, is located on the first floor. The finest view is found at 115 meters on the second floor since you can see the earth below you while diving. At 275 meters, the third level is where you can finally view what Gustave Eiffel's office looked like. It is feasible to utilize the stairs and ascend the steps for the more daring (1,665 to the summit).

To experience the stunning panorama of Paris, you must climb the Eiffel Tower.

2. Cathedral of Notre Dame

One of Paris' most memorable images: The Roman Catholic cathedral Notre-Dame de Paris, often referred to as Notre Dame, is situated on the Ile de la Cité's eastern side. It is generally regarded as one of France and Europe's best examples of French Gothic architecture. This cathedral, which was started in 1163 and finished in 1345, is stunning with its many sculptures and gargoyles that embellish the top.

I suggest that you first take a tour of the cathedral before entering and ascending the 387 steps to the summit of the towers. Although the ascent to the towers' summits may be strenuous, the reward is a panoramic view of the surrounding area and a close-up look at the renowned gargoyles.

3. Musée du Louvre

The Louvre is the world's most popular art gallery. This historic structure, a former royal palace with a total size of 210,000 square meters, including 60,600 exhibits, is located in the center of Paris. The Louvre, where the museum is located, was first a stronghold constructed in the late 12th century under Philip II. In the museum's basement, it is possible to see the fortress's ruins.

There are eight departments in the collection:

Egyptological artifacts

Eastern artifacts

Roman, Greek, and Etruscan

Muslim art

Medieval, Renaissance, and contemporary sculpture

Items of art

Paintings

Graphic design.

4. Champs Elysées and Triumphal Arch

Napoleon asked Jean Chalgrin to create a triumphal arch honoring the valor of the imperial forces after falling under the spell of classical Roman architecture. It is the biggest monument of its sort in the world and was built in the 19th century. Its pillars are adorned with striking sculptures.

Additionally, the top of the arc is inscribed with the names of 558 generals and notable victories. The French Unknown Soldier's Tomb may be found under the Arc de Triomphe.

A lovely view of Paris may be seen from the rooftop patio located over the entrance. The Arc de Triomphe, which is known as "the most magnificent avenue in the world," is situated on the Place de l'Etoile and is 50 meters high, 45 meters wide, and 22 meters deep. It is located 1.9 kilometers from the Arc de Triomphe to the Place de la Concorde. There are several upscale shops (Louis Vuitton, Cartier, Guerlain, Montblanc, etc.), entertainment venues (Lido, movie theaters), and renowned cafés and eateries (Fouquet's).

5. Seine River Cruise

Discover the most effective approach to view the "City of Light" while taking a Seine boat, particularly at night. The monuments are softly illuminated as dusk falls. You get a panoramic perspective, allowing you to take in all of Paris's splendor, including the Eiffel Tower, Notre Dame, Pont Alexandre III, and many more.

Additionally, you may take a boat for a supper cruise on the Seine. You are welcome for roughly two hours.

6. Montmartre

The 130-meter-tall hill in the north of Paris has the name of the district it surrounds. The Basilica of the Sacred Heart, with its white dome at the top, is its most famous feature. It commemorates the French casualties of the Franco-Prussian War of 1870 and was finished in 1919.

Visit the Square of Tertre, which is a few streets from the Basilica, if you're in the region. Many painters have set up their easels to paint visitors or display their work. The Place du Tertre serves as a reminder of the early 20th century period when Montmartre was the center of contemporary art, home to numerous painters like Amedeo Modigliani, Claude Monet, Pablo Picasso, and Vincent van Gogh. A short distance from the Square of Tertre lies the Espace Salvador Dal, a museum devoted mostly to the sculpture and drawings of the Spanish painter.

In Montmartre, you may find the renowned cabaret Moulin Rouge.

7. The Versailles Palace

The most well-known castle in France is Château de Versailles. Versailles was the center of political authority in the Kingdom of France from 1682 until 1789. It was constructed in the 17th century as a representation of French military might and a show of French dominance in Europe. Any traveler who is interested in luxurious lodgings, opulent furnishings, and gilded Renaissance artwork should visit this enormous complex of buildings, gardens, and terraces.

The State Apartments and the renowned Hall of Mirrors, the Queen's room, are where you will begin your tour of Versailles. Remember to take a walk around the renowned "French" gardens.

8. The Luxembourg Park in the Latin Quarter

On the left side of the Seine, close to the Sorbonne, is where you'll find Paris' Latin Quarter. The Latin Quarter is home to various higher education institutions, including the Ecole Normale Superieure, the Ecole des Mines de Paris, and the Ecole

Polytechnique. It is known for its vibrant atmosphere, student life, and bistros. Latin, which was previously widely used at and around the university since it was the dominant language of study across the world in the Middle Ages, gave the region its name.

The Luxembourg Park, a private garden accessible to the general public, was established in 1612 at Marie de Medicis' request to go with the Luxembourg Palace. It is lovingly known as the "Luco" among Parisians. The Palais du Luxembourg, where the Senate meets, is surrounded by a park. You may stroll about the area, which André Le Nôtre redesigned; there is also an orchard, several apple kinds, an apiary, and a greenhouse with an orchid collection. There are 106 sculptures, a figure of Liberty in bronze, and 3 lovely fountains.

9. The Moulin Rouge

The renowned French Cancan is said to have originated in the Moulin Rouge, a cabaret. It was constructed in 1889 by Joseph Oller and Charles Zidler in the center of Pigalle, at the base of the Montmartre slope. The cancan, which was first used as a wooing dance, paved the way for the development of the cabaret, which is now common in many nations worldwide. The Moulin Rouge is now a popular tourist destination that entertains travelers from all over the globe.

Its design and name have been stolen and duplicated from various nightclubs all around the globe, including Las Vegas. The cabaret's renown has also benefited from several movies, including 2001's Baz Luhrmann picture with Nicole Kidman and Ewan McGregor.

10. Paris's Disneyland

A theme park called Disneyland Paris is located near Chessy, France, 32 kilometers (20 miles) east of Paris. Two theme parks, resort hotels, Disney Nature Resorts, a center for eating, entertainment, and shopping, as well as a golf course, are all included.

The complex's first theme park, Disneyland Park, opened its doors in 1992. Walt Disney Studios Park, a second theme park, debuted in 2002. The most popular theme park in Europe, Disneyland Paris celebrated its 25th anniversary in 2017 with 320 million visitors. Following the launch of the Tokyo Disney Resort in 1983, it is the second and biggest Disney park outside of the United States. The Walt Disney Company only owns Disneyland Paris, the only Disney resort outside of the United States.

Mickey enthusiasts may travel 32 kilometers to Disneyland Paris, which has a link to the suburban RER A.

There are two theme parks in Disneyland Paris: Walt Disney Studios and Disneyland, which has the castle from Sleeping Beauty. Big Thunder Mountain, It's a Small World, and Space Mountain are the top attractions.

Having given these Insider's tips on how to enjoy the very best of Paris, I hope this book makes your stay in the city of light a beautiful and memorable one.